Armadillo Trail

The Northward Journey of the Armadillo

Stephen R. Swinburne

Illustrated by Bruce Hiscock

BOYDS MILLS PRESS

HONESDALE, PENNSYLVANIA

Happy Trails!!

Steve Swinburne

2013

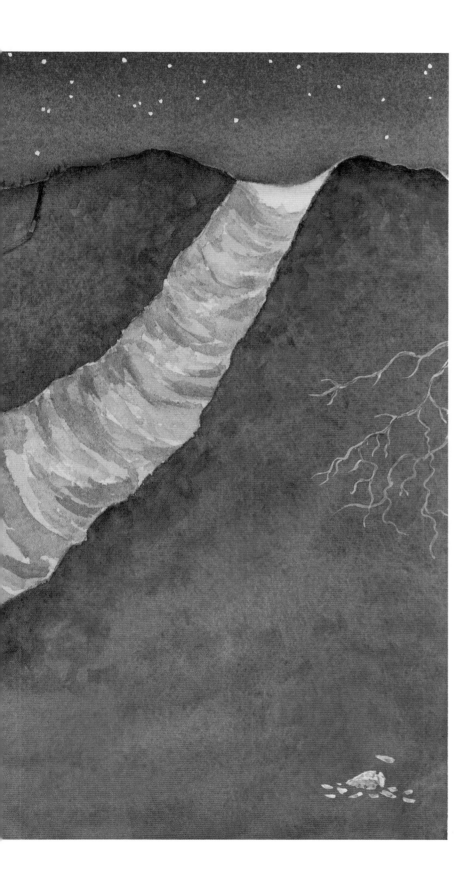

In a cozy hole at the corner of a wide Texas field under a star-spangled night, a mother armadillo gives birth to four babies—all females. The babies are born with their eyes open. A pink and pliable shell covers each of the identical young pups. Within weeks, the quadruplets—armadillos nearly always have four young—test the boundaries of their nest as if ready to explore the world.

A few months later, the mother armadillo leads the way out of the burrow, plowing through the soft mound of leaves, grass, and loose soil. She pokes her nose into the Texas twilight. Her four offspring crowd her shell, sticking their faces above the hole. Hungry and thirsty, she plods away from the burrow. She is a small, armor-plated tank on a search-and-destroy mission. Her quarry—beetles, larvae, flies, ants, earthworms, spiders, slugs, and snails—is any creepy, crawling thing. Her children watch and learn.

With head down, the mother armadillo emits a wheezy, grunting noise. A long snout plows through leaves and debris and probes the soft soil. Her entire head becomes covered in dirt. Powerful front legs with two-inch claws dig while her snout snaps up bugs and earthworms. Her hind legs work like excavators catching the loose dirt and flinging it backward. Hundreds of dirt pilings scatter the field. Armadillos live in great abundance in this Texas pasture.

The mother armadillo moves in short bursts. Dig, burrow, bite. Dig, burrow, bite. Her four babies trail behind, testing their claws in the loosened earth of their mother's wake. Preoccupied with good hunting, she wanders farther and farther from the nest.

Poor eyesight and weak hearing prevent the mother from understanding the danger until it's too late. From across the field, a young farm dog comes bounding into view, barking and snapping at the armadillos. The mother armadillo uses an old trick to escape, darting one way and then another. Three of the young armadillos imitate her tactics and disappear with their mother down the nest hole. But one of the young bolts in the wrong direction and becomes trapped in the open field. The shells on young pups are soft and pliable and vulnerable to predation.

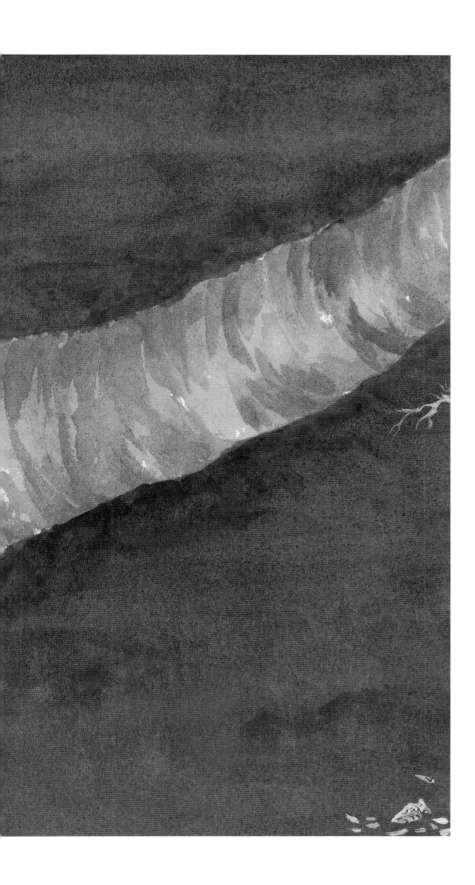

Deep inside the nest, the mother armadillo curls with her frightened pups. The babies nurse. The mother remains alert. The dark hole feels safe, warm, and snug. In the silent space, the armadillo family soon calms and sleeps.

After a long rest, the mother armadillo wakes. She decides to move her family to a new home. The danger of dogs and overcrowding by other armadillos make this habitat unsuitable. Under the cover of nightfall, the family trots across the field, taking a direct path to a tangle of briars. The mother follows the edge of the floodplain of a small river. She knows the soil is loose and easy to burrow. She plods on steadily, wandering back and forth from the damp earth beside the freshwater marsh to higher ground in the woodlands. Occasionally she stands upright on hind legs, balancing on her tail, to sniff the air. The habitat feels right to her. Beetles and ants scurry in the woodland leaf litter while worms and leeches wriggle in the mud. Her long, sticky tongue slurps up all of these tasty morsels.

Over the long summer and into autumn, mother armadillo digs eight burrows throughout the low and high ground of the river basin. These holes make safe places for her family to hide and rest. Her three pups grow quickly, their armor plates hardening as tough as tree bark. At two months, the armadillo pups begin to eat insects, and by three months, they are weaned—no more mother's milk. It's bugs and beetles for breakfast, lunch, and dinner for the armadillo family.

One of the three young armadillos, the largest of her offspring, seems bolder, more alert. Each day the big female explores farther and farther from her mother's side. On a warm August evening, the big female wanders away from her mother and the other pups. She walks north, keeping the river to one side and the insect-rich woods to the other.

She knows where to find water. She knows where to root for food. When tired of walking, she digs a hole to sleep. If threatened, she'll locate a burrow to hide in. Sometimes she finds abandoned armadillo burrows and stays for a day or two. She moves at night, wandering at will, letting the river guide her general direction. When she walks out of Texas and scuttles across the border into Oklahoma, she neither knows nor cares. She is Texas-born, but she has a traveling soul.

On a cloudy afternoon in late August, where the river valley meets a highway, the big female is drawn to a delicious smell. She scampers up to the edge of the road, stands on her hind legs, and squints across the pavement. Her nose draws her forward. A freshly killed opossum rests along the double yellow line in the middle of the road. The armadillo nudges the carcass with her snout. She tastes the carrion.

Like all armadillos, her eyesight is weak, her hearing is better, but she relies mostly on a keen sense of smell. A red pickup truck rumbles near, missing her by inches. Startled, the armadillo springs two feet in the air. She lands on all fours and dashes from the road. Leaping into the air when surprised acts to startle a predator. This behavior gives an armadillo a chance to scurry to the safety of a den.

The armadillo keeps running until she pauses at the edge of a small pond. She gulps a lot of air to inflate her lungs, stomach, and intestines and, with a body as round as an inner tube, dog-paddles away from the shore. When she reaches the middle of the pond, she belches out the air from her stomach and sinks like a hammer. The armadillo plops to the bottom of the pond and walks underwater. Like a submarine with legs, the armadillo plows forward, stepping over water plants, squinting at fish. She can hold her breath in her lungs for up to six minutes. She emerges on the other side and scrambles up the bank. The sun breaks through and the heat forces the armadillo underground. She crawls into an old foxhole and sleeps.

Weather controls the armadillo's life in the days and weeks ahead. During hot days, the armadillo curls deep inside the cool dens and burrows she's dug or found. When the temperature falls, the big female probes the southern night with her beady eyes and bug-slurping snout.

By early winter, the big female has wandered farther into Oklahoma. A mild season allows the armadillo to stay active. She emerges at the hottest time of the day and forages for bugs. She meets other armadillos. She sometimes shares the same den with females.

The big female follows the wide river valleys and quiet highways of western Oklahoma. She keeps plodding and plowing and pushing north, never really finding what she is looking for. What is the big female armadillo looking for? She'll know when she finds it.

For two years, her northward meandering has taken her far, far away from the crowded nest hole in Texas with mother armadillo and her siblings.

As a full moon rises over a low hill on a June evening just outside Liberal, Kansas, the big female meets a young male armadillo. After mating, and almost eight months to the day on a late February afternoon, the female huddles in her leafy nest and gives birth to four identical newborns. Loosely packed soil stuffed with snails and slugs makes this Kansas hillside a perfect habitat. The big female digs many burrows, lining them with dry grasses and leaves. She's found home.

28

Her four female pups stay with her for almost a year until, one early spring day, the largest of her pups walks away and slowly shuffles north.

About Armadillos

Armadillos are like pocket-sized dinosaurs. Along with sloths and anteaters, armadillos belong in a group of mammals called xenarthrans. Members of the xenarthra (*zen-AR-thra*) group of animals have similar characteristics, such as few or no teeth, a small brain, and a jointed back that provides extra strength for digging. The common ancestor of armadillos, sloths, and anteaters evolved about 55 million years ago in South America. When the Spanish came to the New World, they called this animal *el armadillo*, "the little armored one." Today, there are twenty species of armadillo that inhabit the Western Hemisphere, and only one, the nine-banded armadillo, lives in the United States.

A stiff and leathery armor covers the armadillo's back, tail, and head. The animal's underbelly, however, is not protected and consists of skin and fur. Although the shell, or carapace, on a young armadillo resembles human fingernail material, the adult armadillo's shell hardens into thin bone. The flexible bands in the middle of its armored shell allow the armadillo to bend and maneuver. If you've spotted a nine-banded armadillo, don't expect to count nine bands, as they may have anywhere from six to eleven movable bands on their shells.

Most armadillos in the northern and southern sections of their range have eight bands, while those in the more central areas possess nine. Count the number of bands on the armadillo illustrated in the book. Are there eight or nine?

If an adult nine-banded armadillo is the size of a house cat, the young armadillo is the size of a kitten. While it is true that the nine-banded armadillo nearly always has four identical pups, either male or female, these armadillos sometimes give birth to three or even five young. Armadillos weigh on average between nine and sixteen pounds, and they can live for twelve to fifteen years. Although nine-banded armadillos cannot, as often believed, roll themselves up into a tight ball for protection, three-banded armadillos from South America are capable of this strategy.

In 1971, scientists discovered that armadillos are one of the few animals other than man to contract leprosy. Armadillos have proved very valuable to medical researchers in learning about this deadly disease, and this knowledge has helped scientists to develop a vaccine to protect against leprosy.

Armadillos are on the move! Believe it or not, no nine-banded armadillos lived in the United States before 1850. What prevented armadillos from invading the country? They couldn't get across large

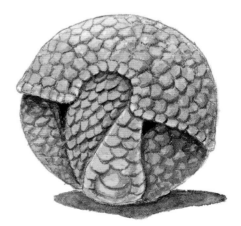

Unlike the nine-banded armadillo, the three-banded armadillo of South America can roll itself into a ball for protection.

rivers like the Rio Grande and the Mississippi. And even if some made it, predators such as wolves, grizzlies, and mountain lions were waiting for them. Native Americans ate them, too.

But after 1850, one of the fastest expansions of any mammal species was about to begin. As waves of settlers moved west, populations of both Indians and large predators were reduced. Forests were transformed into fields and farms, better habitat for armadillos. Human traffic across rivers increased the chances of armadillos hitching rides.

They were first recorded along the Rio Grande in southern Texas in 1854. San Antonio residents sighted armadillos by 1880. Austin had armadillos by 1914, Abilene by 1945, Dallas by 1953. Escaped pairs from a zoo in 1922 and a circus truck in 1936 began a new migrating population in Florida. Armadillos from Texas and Florida have migrated north and now occupy Alabama, Arkansas, Colorado, Georgia, Kansas, Kentucky, Illinois, Louisiana, Mississippi, Missouri, Nebraska, North Carolina, South Carolina, Oklahoma, New Mexico, and Tennessee. They've even been seen as far north as Indiana. Some biologists predict armadillos might reach Pennsylvania, New York, Ohio, Massachusetts, and Rhode Island.

Armadillos cannot tolerate cold northern winters, as they have very little fur to keep them warm. Cold weather (average January temperature for these animals needs to be above 28 degrees Fahrenheit) and lack of rain will stop the armadillo march from heading too far north or west. But you never know how far this miniature bug-eating tank will travel, so keep your eyes peeled.

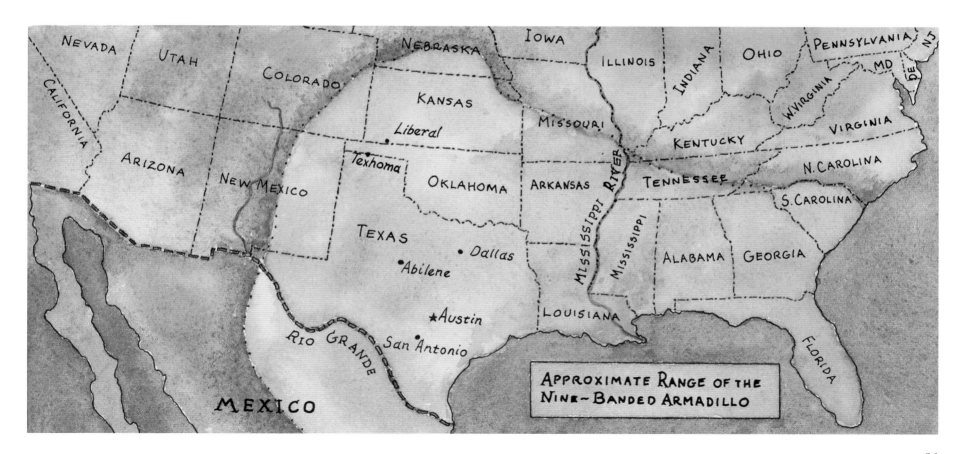

APPROXIMATE RANGE OF THE NINE-BANDED ARMADILLO

To the scintillating Texas librarians and teachers I've met over the years, including Gary Brown, Alison Crittenden, Bonnie Fowler, Aileen Kirkham, and Vicki Krebsbach. Y'all know how to put the right book in a child's hands.
—S.S.

To the memory of my stepbrother, Raun Smith, and also to his son Justin
—B.H.

The author wishes to thank the following individuals for their gracious assistance: Joyce E. Hofmann, Ph.D., senior research scientist–mammalogist and curator of the Illinois Natural History Survey Mammal Collection; Joshua Nixon, Ph.D., Biology Department, University of Minnesota; and John Young, mammalogist, Texas Parks and Wildlife Department.

Boyds Mills Press, Inc.
815 Church Street
Honesdale, Pennsylvania 18431
Printed in China

Library of Congress Cataloging-in-Publication Data

Swinburne, Stephen R.
  Armadillo trail : the northward journey of the Armadillo / Stephen R. Swinburne ;
  Illustrated by Bruce Hiscock. — 1st ed.
      p. cm.
  ISBN 978-1-59078-463-1 (hardcover : alk. paper)
  1. Armadillos—Juvenile literature. I. Hiscock, Bruce, ill. II. Title.
  QL737.E23S95 2008
  599.3'12—dc22
                              2008028774

First edition
The text of this book is set in 13-point Clearface.
The illustrations are done in watercolor.

10 9 8 7 6 5 4 3 2 1